Welcome

Welcome to one of the more extraordir
earth. Through the ages, St Michael's M
spiritual centre, a military stronghold, a thriving port and a
much loved family home. It attracts archaeologists, artists and
art critics, geologists, historians, horticulturists, musicians and
pilgrims. Others are drawn by the beauty of the place or for
the challenge of the climb or to sample the wonderful views.

In 1954, my grandfather gave most of the island to the National Trust together with a
large endowment fund to support its future running costs. At the same time it was agreed
that the family would hold a 999 year lease to live in the castle and a licence to operate
the visitor business. Consequently my family continues to run the island on a daily basis,
as we have been doing for 350 years, but its long term future is underpinned by the
National Trust.

I moved onto the Mount in the autumn of 2003, together with my wife, Mary and our
children following the retirement of my uncle, Lord St Levan, to the mainland. It is an
unusual place to live but we love the many contrasting moods of this wonderful island
through the seasons of the year.

In the first and main part of this booklet, the text follows the route you will take round
the castle, and I have included points of interest that I might have mentioned if I had been
accompanying you in person. The castle's long history means that there are various layers
of history that overlay each other from the distant past until the present day. At the end
of the booklet is a timeline of major events and a list of members of my family who have
occupied the Mount.

You might imagine that the story of somewhere like this would all be tidily documented.
In practice, new information and perspectives about the Mount's history, both recent
and long ago, are constantly emerging. Please feel free to discuss with our guides any
questions or comments that you yourself may have.

I hope that you enjoy your visit and want to come back to see us again soon.

James St Aubyn

On the way to the castle

As you go past the Checkpoint to start your tour, there is a small herb garden on your left. It is likely that the monks in medieval times would have grown herbs on St Michael's Mount for cooking and for medicinal purposes, and all of the herbs here would have been available to them then.

On the way to the castle

When I was a boy, the picnic area on the right was a tennis court, which we used often in the summer holidays. In those days the castle was open only three days a week so our mis-hits were only sometimes witnessed by passing visitors.

Ahead lies an attractive Victorian building, which was designed as a dairy, while being a miniature copy of the kitchens of Glastonbury Abbey. For some twenty five years until 1909, a small herd of Jersey cows were kept on the Mount to provide for the needs of the island.

As the slope begins to rise more steeply, you climb the Pilgrim Steps, which were uncovered in my grandfather's time. They are early enough to have been used by medieval pilgrims, although you might have expected their route to have led directly from the causeway.

At the top of the Pilgrim Steps, a wooden ladder on your right takes you up to the Cornish Cross Garden, a commanding view at any time and gorgeous when the camellias are in flower. From here you can see various small headstones in the pets' cemetery, dated between 1891 and 1923. One inscription reads *SHOT died 8 July 1905* which hopefully refers to an animal's name rather than its manner of dispatch. Another is more worthy: *Billy – May our lives be simply true as thine.*

During the English Civil War, this whole enclosure would have been part of the defensive system to protect the island when it was under siege. Further up the main cobbled path, there is another Civil War fortification on your left with beautiful vertical stonework typical of the period.

This was the site of a gun platform built in the 1640s. There would also have been a gateway across the path to protect the Well, which would have been the main source of water at that time.

The Well is also the focal point of one of the most famous legends about St Michael's Mount. Deep in the mists of time, before there were any buildings, a giant called Cormoran is said to have lived in a cave at the top of the rock. Cormoran caused great disruption on the mainland, stealing hens, lambs, pigs and even the occasional stray child to fill his prodigious appetite. When everyone else had despaired of controlling the giant, a young lad called Jack came up with a cunning plan.

"For some twenty five years until 1909, a small herd of Jersey cows were kept on the Mount to provide for the needs of the island."

The Dairy

Jack the Giant Killer

Vertical Stonework

Did you know?

There are a number of natural springs on the island, these were the water supply for the island up until 100 years ago.

The Giants Heart

He came across the causeway by night and dug a deep hole where the Well now is. He covered it over with branches and leaves to disguise his trap, and when dawn came he roused the sleeping giant from his deep slumber. Now Cormoran was furious to be disturbed and before he had properly woken up, he chased after Jack, stumbling as the sun was in his eyes. Jack ran round the concealed pit, but Cormoran did not notice his danger and down the hole he plunged.

Further up the cobbled path, it is still possible to see the giant's heart. Do not be fooled by the large stone by the side of the track. A giant's heart is tiny and rather dark. You can spot it by your feet among the cobbles.

Next you will come to a watchtower and defensive wall on your right and the remains of a guardroom on your left. Between them would have been another gateway. Notice the Murdering Hole in the defensive wall. When the enemy was at the gate, a musket fired through this would have been lethal.

Although built on the site of an earlier set of buildings, these structures were part of the Civil War defences. It would have been possible to fire on attackers in the harbour area from the sentry box.

Avoid the temptation to take a short cut up to the entrance, but walk round to the imposing rows of cannons facing west. Replacing earlier smaller gun emplacements, the present batteries were probably installed in the late 18th century, mainly for ceremonial purposes to salute an important guest or to be fired on special occasions. Nevertheless they were serviceable enough for serious action against a French frigate during the Napoleonic Wars.

The gap starting between the gun batteries and running down to the base of the island is called Cromwell's Passage, and this is the hazardous route that Parliamentarian troops are said to have used to try to take the garrison by surprise. However the ploy was unsuccessful and the invaders were repulsed (the armour of some of the casualties can be seen in the room called Chevy Chase later in the tour).

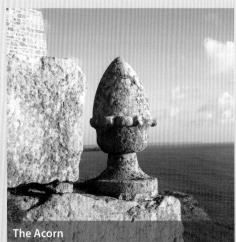
The Acorn

The Sentry Box

Did you know?

During the Civil War it would have been possible to fire on attackers in the harbour area from the sentry box.

The Murdering Hole

On the left-hand of the two cliffs defining Cromwell's Passage is where St Michael is said to have appeared in 495 to warn fishermen off the rocks. St Michael was an important figure in early medieval times. Often pictured with scales in his hands, he was thought to determine whether departing souls went to Heaven or Hell, and churches dedicated to him were often built in high places to reflect his status as the mediator between God and Man.

As you start to make your way towards the West Door of the castle, you will pass a curious acorn shaped stone statue. As children we used to speculate that it was a boiled egg but one of our guides recently spotted it in an old drawing in the Long Passage as an ornamental feature on the roof of the recently converted Blue Drawing Room. Quite possibly the acorn was moved here at a later date because it became unstable.

The way to the West Door would have been the only approach to the castle before the Victorian East Wing (where we now live) was built. Even in monastic times, the entrance would have been guarded, and once the Mount assumed greater military importance, this part of the castle would have accommodated the Captain of the Mount and his soldiers.

The two protruding towers may originally have been the same size, but the left hand one was expanded during the reign of Henry VIII as part of his policy of strengthening the coastal defences all along the South Coast. The West Door itself is also Tudor and must have replaced an earlier entrance. An additional storey with attic windows was added as part of the Victorian restoration to provide more staff bedrooms. It has now been partly converted to be an open space where our children have their pool table and can entertain friends a safe distance from their parents.

Entrance Hall

When the priory was first built, the Entrance Hall area may have been the room where justice was administered to those who had committed misdemeanours on monastic lands. By the end of the twelfth century, in 1193, the priory had been captured by Henry de Pomeray overpowering the monks. This was during the period when the future King John was flexing his muscles while his brother, Richard the Lionheart, was held in captivity on the continent during his journey back from the Third Crusade. Whilst de Pomeray's tenure was short-lived, the Mount was recognised from then on as a military as well as a religious stronghold.

The remains of a fifteenth century cannon in the glass case by the window were found outside the West Door. During the Wars of the Roses, the Earl of Oxford captured the Mount in 1473 and held it for six months under siege. The foremost nobleman in Cornwall, Sir Henry Arundell, was commanded to remove the Earl. Arundell was reluctant because a prophecy had indicated that he would die on a beach, and so it happened that an arrow in his eye felled him on the sands of Marazion.

Eventually the Earl of Oxford surrendered. He remained in exile until his return with the future Henry VII, for whom he commanded the right flank at the decisive Battle of Bosworth.

The castle also saw the steel of battle during the Civil War, and was one of the last Royalist strongholds. Following its surrender, my ancestor, Colonel St Aubyn, a parliamentarian, was appointed Governor of the Mount in 1647 and tasked with keeping the peace in the surrounding area on the mainland. Twelve years later he purchased the Mount from the Bassett family, who had been temporarily impoverished by their support of the King.

In particular, the colossal sums spent in fortifying the Mount were recorded by Lady Ann Bassett as executor of her husband's Will. By the west wall, you can see Colonel St Aubyn's travelling trunk inscribed with his name and the date 1663.

Despite the popular perception of Cornwall as a Royalist county, its gentry were in fact fairly evenly divided between the two causes. As the theologian Richard Baxter commented *"the King hath the better cause, but Parliament hath the better men"*. While John St Aubyn was a parliamentarian, his brother Thomas was a Royalist. The Colonel's father-in-law, Francis Godolphin of Treveneague, was for Parliament while his cousins, the charismatic Sir Francis and Sidney Godolphin of Godolphin were dashing cavaliers.

Although the antagonism between the supporters of King and Parliament was intense, it did not match the depth of the Cornish people's loyalty to their county and each other. As a result few outrages were committed among the Cornish themselves and the end of hostilities, when it came, was relatively bloodless.

In contrast to some other parts of the country, the Civil War left little lasting resentment in Cornwall. For instance, it is perhaps interesting to note that, less than a hundred years after his family had been compelled for financial reasons to sell the Mount, the then Francis Basset of Tehidy would marry Margaret St Aubyn, the Colonel's great great granddaughter.

The decorative coat of arms by the chimney and beautiful plasterwork round the walls were commissioned by the Colonel's son, the first Sir John St Aubyn. It was moved during the Victorian restoration from the room above, an extraordinarily delicate undertaking.

As you leave the Entrance Hall there is a small picture of an elderly man elegantly dressed in black. This is the first Lord St Levan, soon after he was made a peer in 1887. He spent over £100,000, a fortune in the 1870s, building the East Wing of the castle as well as transforming the village from a sprawling collection of buildings, many in a considerable state of disrepair, to what now exists by the harbour.

Right – Colonel St Aubyn's Trunk

Left – Coat of Arms
The St Aubyn arms on the left; the arms of Ann Jenkin of St Columb, wife of the 1st Baronet, on the right .The St Aubyn family motto *In Se Teres,* roughly translated as complete or rounded in himself, is an extract from the description of a moral man in Horace's Satires.

Sir John's Room

This southwest wing of the castle was added in the mid sixteenth century after the Reformation, when the castle was occupied as a single unit and it made sense to join the previously separate west (military) and south (religious) ranges of the castle buildings. Until the renovations of the 1870s it was a kitchen, and during recent building work we found a waste hole in the west wall full of broken china, ancient chicken bones and the like.

The partners' desk in the centre of the room can be detached into three sections, and is said to have been taken round the agricultural estate on the mainland for the collection of rents. Notice the lettering on the drawers which indicates a rather basic filing system.

Above – Portrait of James St Aubyn
English School portrait of James St Aubyn, oldest son of the 5th Sir John, who inherited the Mount on his father's death in 1839. He and his wife, Sarah, had three daughters, and after him, the Mount and estate passed to his half-brother, Edward.

Right – Tidal clock
In the summer we have to adjust for the fact that BST did not exist when the clock was made.

As well as the hour of the day, the grandfather clock in the corner shows when the tide will be at high water. The times of the tide are important to anyone who lives on St Michael's Mount to calculate when the causeway will be open. Either side of the clock are small portraits of the 3rd Sir John and his wife, Catherine. He was known for his integrity. Sir Robert Walpole said of him – *Every man hath his price save that little Cornish baronet.* Many St Aubyns have been called John. Following Colonel St Aubyn, himself a John, the next five generations were all called Sir John, after the creation of the baronetcy in 1671.

The portrait on the left of the exit door is of the 5th Sir John as an old man. He inherited from his father at the age of 14 and died at 82 so that he had a long spell at the helm of the family fortunes. He was an avid collector of books, pictures, botanical and geological specimens, as well as the medieval stained glass you will see in Chevy Chase and the Chapel. He was also an inveterate gambler, and one night at his club Brooks's lost a farm, then on the outskirts of London, on which much of Putney has since been built.

His personal life was equally colourful. According to an account by the diarist, Joseph Farington, Sir John spent three years as a young man in Paris and whilst spreading his wild oats formed a connection with an Italian lady by whom he had a natural daughter. Back in Cornwall, he lived for several years with Martha Nicholls by whom he had a further five children without marrying her. Martha was the daughter of John Nicholls, a respected landscape gardener who worked on the grounds at Clowance, which had been the principal St Aubyn family home since the fourteenth century. When this relationship ended, Sir John settled Martha in nearby Ludgvan with an allowance, and by all accounts he remained very fond of her.

Sir John's final relationship was with Juliana Vinicombe, daughter of a yeoman farmer from Marazion, by whom he had a further nine children, but only after all these had been born did Sir John marry Juliana in 1822. Overall they stayed together for over 45 years until Sir John died in 1839, and Juliana's influence, as well as his, is still discernible on the Mount.

One consequence of Sir John's unconventional approach towards matrimony, as a result of which he had no legitimate heirs, was that the traditional family seat at Clowance passed under entail to the son of his sister Catherine. (Originally the Reverend John Molesworth, he took the surname Molesworth St Aubyn, which his descendants at Pencarrow in North Cornwall retain today). Another consequence was that the baronetcy became extinct, although a new baronetcy was created in 1866 for his son, Edward. Sir John also left sizeable debts, but the family fortunes had revived sufficiently by the 1870s for his grandson to embark on his major conversion of the castle.

The modern portrait by the entrance is of my grandfather, who gave St Michael's Mount to the National Trust. This room was not open to the public in his time as he kept it as his study. Occasionally I come here in the evenings and there is a wonderful feeling of the world being put to rest watching from the window as the sun sets in the west.

Above – Mantlepiece clock
Made by Thomas Mudge, one of England's most outstanding clockmakers. In 1757, he invented the lever escapement, which was a signal advance in the way pocket watches were made. In 1776 Mudge was appointed watchmaker to the King. When he retired to Plymouth with ill health, Mudge handed over his business in London to the Dutton family, one of whose clocks was in the previous room.

Left – Portrait of Edward St Aubyn as a boy
By John Opie, Edward succeeded his half-brother James. By then he was 63 and suffered from neuralgia, so remained at his home in Devonport, where he already managed the family's extensive properties. His son, John, became the first Lord St Levan.

Ante Room

The main feature in this small room is the collection of miniatures contained in the cabinet on your left as you enter. Before the age of photography, the gift of a miniature was a charming means of providing a lover or loved one with an image by which to be remembered. Miniatures would sometimes contain some other personal keepsake.

1. Juliana Vinicombe – English School
Later Lady St Aubyn.

2. Sir John St Aubyn, 5th Baronet – Phyllis Jessup
And a sample of Sir John's hair.

3. Lady in blue – Jeremiah Meyer

4. Sir Thomas Williamson – Artist unknown
Thomas was created a baronet by Charles I for his fidelity to the King. He was the great grandfather of Elizabeth Wingfield, wife of the 4th Sir John.

5. Lord Edward Howard – Nicholas Dixon
Younger brother of the 6th Duke of Norfolk. Attributed to Nicholas Dixon who in 1673 was appointed Limner to Charles II.

6. Lady in blue – John Hoskins
This may be Margaret Lemon, Van Dyke's model and mistress. She was famously extravagant both in her passions and spending.

7. Charles I – Artist unknown
The question is whether this was painted in 1642 or 1648.

8. Lady Anne Clifford – Peter Oliver
The daughter of an Earl, she married the Earls of Dorset and then Pembroke. A strong character, she was the maternal grandmother of Catherine Morice, wife of the third Sir John. Attributed to Peter Oliver.

9. Young lady in white cap – James Nixon

10. Lady Lucy Morice – Jacques-Antoine Arlaud
Sister of Catherine, Lady St Aubyn.

For instance, at the foot of the cabinet, the reverse side of one is shown to reveal a lock of hair from the 5th Sir John St Aubyn. (The front shows a portrait very similar to the neighbouring image of him.)

The five miniatures at the top of the cabinet are all from the seventeenth century. The central one of Charles I is something of a mystery. On the back is a hand written inscription *"Sat for by the King for Sir Bevil Grenville 1642"*. Bevil Grenville was extremely popular in Cornwall, and played a distinguished part in the famous victories at Braddock Down and Stratton before leading his Royalist forces on a bold march through Devon and Somerset. He was finally defeated and killed at Lansdowne, near Bath in 1643. The Cornish were never so united after his death.

So it is entirely plausible that Charles I would have given the miniature to Sir Bevil but the mystery is why the King's beard was so long and untidy. There is another portrait of him with an unkempt beard, but this was painted shortly before his execution in 1649, when the imprisoned monarch was no longer allowed the services of the royal barber. Clearly, if the portrait is from that period, the sitting could not have been for Sir Bevil Grenville.

We are also not certain who painted the two large panoramic views of St Michael's Mount on the adjacent wall. They date from the late seventeenth or early eighteenth century and were copied by Samuel and Nathaniel Buck when publishing their prints of the Mount. Samuel Buck, either on his own or with his brother Nathaniel,

produced a comprehensive series of prints of monuments and views throughout England and Wales. One of their two prints of the Mount is on the wall opposite.

Just before you leave the room, take a look at the stormy scene by Paul Sandby, perhaps the most prominent early painter of watercolours in this country. This picture was given to St Michael's Mount by A.L.Rowse, academic and historian, a Cornishman who was equally at home in his native county or at All Souls College in Oxford. A.L.Rowse's mother had worked for a time as a housemaid in St Michael's Mount and he had a great fondness for the place.

4.

5.

8.

9.

6.

7.

10.

Library

This room formed part of the twelfth century monastic buildings. It was converted to its present format in the 1780s when the ceiling was introduced and a bedroom created in a new room immediately above (with the same elegant south facing windows). Before that it was one tall room, most likely the monks' kitchen with a chimney to release smoke from cooking. It is set back from the rooms to the east, possibly to minimise the danger of fire spreading, while the two rooms you have just left were only added in the sixteenth century after the reformation of the monasteries.

A religious community may have been first established on St Michael's Mount any time from as early as the sixth century as the cult of St Michael spread through Europe.

By the eleventh century, the island and various landholdings on the mainland had come under the control of Mont-St-Michel in Normandy. Under the supervision of Bernard Le Bec, then Abbot of the Mont, the construction of the new priory buildings started in 1135. These stone buildings may have replaced an earlier wooden structure. Bernard Le Bec, also known as Bernard the Builder, was responsible for founding several other daughter priories of Mont-St-Michel in Normandy. These have a distinctive lay out where each room has its place, and although the architecture of this priory would have been constrained by the structure of the rock on St Michael's Mount, Bernard's house style gives some helpful hints to how the priory might have been laid out here.

One theory is that the Abbots of Mont-St-Michel used this outpost as a testing ground for young monks, on the basis that if they survived five years or so of Cornish winters on the island, they would have the fortitude to pursue their religious calling for the rest of their lives. Mont-St-Michel's control over its Cornish possessions weakened during the Hundred Years War with France, and its ownership was finally severed in 1414. Then, as part of his confiscation of alien priories (that is any religious establishment with an overseas parentage), Henry V gave St Michael's Mount to Syon Abbey, his new foundation at Twickenham in London.

Nowadays, we are good friends with colleagues at Mont-St-Michel, and they have been particularly interested in the watercolours in this room, which date from the 1820s and are views of the Normandy Mont and its Bay. The scenes of the interior are the only known record of what the Mont looked like at that time. For a long while I wondered why the figures in the Abbey were lounging around in a seemingly disrespectful way, until I discovered that during the Napoleonic Wars and for a period afterwards the Mont had been converted to a prison. The poor incumbents no doubt had every reason to look bored.

The watercolours were painted by John Cole, steward to the 5th Sir John St Aubyn.

A recently identified extract from documents held at the University of Glasgow suggest that Sir John had ambitions to reunite the two Mounts by taking advantage of the collapse of property prices in France following Napoleon's defeat. The clue arises in a letter dated 7 October 1828 from Rear Admiral Charles Fielding to his stepson, describing an extensive visit to Cornwall, a passage of which reads "– *thence on to St Michael's Mount to St John St Aubyns – which is a very interesting place where we sleep. By the bye St John just missed buying some Time since the other Mont St Michel in Granville Bay – it would have been curious to have been the possessor of both. he would have had some difficulty in tunnelling a road from one to the other*".

Meanwhile, as it is designed now, this room has a charming intimate feel, which might seem unexpected in its castle environment. Among the furniture, it is worth noting the brass inlaid mahogany chairs either side of the gaming table which are part of a set made by John Channon of London, a contemporary of Chippendale.

Oposite page left top– Gaming Table
The rosewood gaming table dates from c.1840 and attributed to the Lancastrian furniture makers, Gillows, whose merger in 1897 with Waring of Liverpool created the well known firm of Waring and Gillow.

Oposite page left – John Channon Chair
From his workshops in St Martin's Lane, John Channon was the leading manufacturer of brass inlaid furniture between 1730 and 1760. Given the family's penchant for the Rococo style, it is not surprising that Channon's chairs should be here.

Chevy Chase

Our guides are sometimes asked if this room is called after the American actor of the same name, but in reality it is a loose punning reference between the medieval ballad, Chevy Chase, and the hunting scenes in the plaster frieze that runs all round the room.

The frieze was created at some time between the late sixteenth and mid seventeenth century, and shows assorted animals being pursued, including a representation of an ostrich above the southwest window where the artist has decided to incorporate a horseshoe as part of the animal's mouth.

In Norman times, this would have been the monks' refectory. Beneath it would have been the priory's main storeroom (now the Garrison Room) and, had Bernard Le Bec been able to follow his usual design, above would have been the monks' dormitory. However it is debatable whether such a top-heavy structure would have been viable on this site and it is possible that the monks slept elsewhere. After the dissolution of the monasteries, the room was reconstructed in the sixteenth century as the Great Hall of the castle.

The main timbers in the roof date from this period as does the small arched door by the entrance. The glass floor through this door reveals winder stairs to the Garrison Room below. This would have been an external staircase with a courtyard beyond it until the Victorian renovations. These created new kitchens on the far side of the castle and installed the kitchen stairs and serving hatch to enable food to be brought to Chevy Chase, which remained the main dining room in the castle until the 1950s. My father could remember being served here as a boy by footmen in canary yellow uniforms, and even now on some special occasions we have a formal meal or hold a reception in Chevy Chase. At our Christmas Party, a children's entertainer performs in here, just as one did when I was a child.

In my grandparent's time, there was still an indoor staff of fourteen, including a butler and two footmen, although by then the butler was soberly dressed in black morning dress and the footmen wore grey suits. When my uncle took over in the mid nineteen seventies, this complement was streamlined considerably, as indeed it still is today. We have a Castle Steward, who lives in a flat within the castle, and has a wide range of responsibilities to ensure the smooth running of the place. Then there are two permanent conservation assistants, increasing to three in the summer, who come in the mornings mainly to prepare the public rooms in the season or for more specialist work in the winter. Finally our Housekeeper, who comes over from the mainland four mornings a week, helps make sure that our private quarters are kept on an even keel.

The long table was introduced by my uncle, the 4th Lord St Levan. In order to reach Chevy Chase, it had to be carried up the Mount and brought through the castle. Luckily the top comes away from the legs or the table would never have made the journey intact. It used to be the practice with refectory tables like this to turn the top over every six months or so to use both sides evenly, and this is meant to have given rise to the phrase *turning the tables*.

A rather fascinating piece is the triangular Elizabethan chair in the far corner. It was brought to the Mount in 1690 by Francis St Aubyn, Mayor of Marazion, who lived here while his older brother John resided in the original family house at Clowance. The chair was made by a Bodger or a traditional woodworker who used a tree lathe to produce its legs, sides and back. The power for the lathe was generated by the force of a bent bough of a tree springing back to its original position. Unlike a modern lathe this operation rarely made two articles alike and in due course Bodgers Chairs gave birth to the modern expression of a *Bodge Job*.

1.   2.

A special feature of this room is the beautiful stained glass in the relatively sheltered windows on the north side. These include samples of Dutch, English, Flemish and French work which were collected by the 5th Sir John and probably acquired from private chapels and oratories. There are some especially fine examples in the window in the middle. At the lowest level are two roundels depicting Heaven and Hell, with St Peter welcoming the Elect on one side and hell devils dragging the damned to their fate on the other. These are Flemish and date from about 1500. Just above, from the same period, are *"The three living and the three dead"* showing three young dandies being warned of the error of their ways by three of the recently deceased. Curiously a similar image can be found at Mont-St-Michel.

In the alcove round the corner is a selection of our family silver. This largely dates from the eighteenth century as successive generations continued the conversion of the castle from a military garrison to a more comfortable private home. When the castle is closed on Christmas Day, I borrow from this cabinet and for a short time our own

dining table glows with the lovely George II candlesticks, the George III sauce boats and the William III porringer. Meanwhile, if you glance up to the right, you will see our oldest single piece of stained glass in the castle, a coat of arms with a rampant lion on a dark blue background. This is French from about 1450 although, when they were much younger, my children would claim that it was the emblem of Gryffindor in Harry Potter.

The portraits are of sixteenth or seventeenth century characters, among which is George Monck who showed enormous diplomacy, nerve and skill as the person most responsible for negotiating the peaceful restoration of Charles II to the throne. In local terms, Colonel St Aubyn was one of thirty seven Cornish gentlemen who sat in Truro between 27 and 31 December 1659 to consider the state of the county and concluded by issuing a public proclamation

in favour of a Free Parliament, the first step towards the return of the king. This early Cornish support for Monck's efforts was influential in paving the way for the Restoration the following year.

To celebrate the new status quo, Colonel St Aubyn installed the Royal coat of arms in plaster, above the fireplace. On the opposite wall are the arms of the St Aubyn family impaling the double-headed eagle of the Godolphin family, of whom his wife Catherine was a member.

On the far wall, as you look back are pieces of armour found on the island, possibly from fallen parliamentary soldiers who tried to capture the Mount coming up Cromwell's Passage. Certainly one helmet bears evidence of a blow likely to have proved fatal. By the window is a seventeenth century leather jug. It is perfectly normal in itself, but what is special is that it was found in a secret chamber under the Chapel with a very tall skeleton. But more of that story later.

Above – Stained glass
Stained glass roundels from the central window.

Detail of frieze

Detail of frieze

Detail of oak chair – head of Suzanna

Detail of chair back

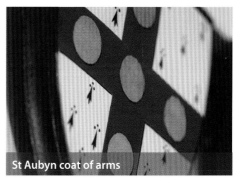

St Aubyn coat of arms

Above – Armour
Mid 17th century pikesman's armour found on the west side of the island.
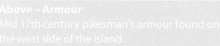

Smoking Room

This room was overhauled during the Victorian renovations, with the north and east walls rebuilt and the bay window inserted in the south wall. It is called the Smoking Room because it was here gentlemen would retire to smoke their cigars and drink port after dining in Chevy Chase. In its original construction under the auspices of Bernard Le Bec, this would have been the Prior's day room or office, while he would have had his own bedroom above and his personal storeroom below, where confidential documents could be kept secure.

The room above is now known as the King Charles Room as it is believed that Charles II, when Prince of Wales, slept here before fleeing to the Isles of Scilly on the night of 2nd March 1646.

This is highly likely as Sir Arthur Bassett, who had inherited St Michael's Mount on his brother's death the previous September, was one of the Prince's three companions on the voyage, apart that is from his personal retinue. Unfortunately the access to this room is too narrow to show it, but you will be able to see it from outside from the terrace.

Meanwhile the Prior's storeroom is now my cellar. So, if you happen to hear the clanking of bottles underfoot, you can assume that I am searching for a suitable wine for guests. One of the quirky aspects of our life here is that we live in an upside down house. The lower floors of our East Wing are mainly given to bedrooms while the top floor houses our drawing room, dining room and kitchen. Finally I have to climb another flight of stairs to reach the cellar, which is wonderfully cool, nestled into the rock.

The picture over the fireplace shows the first Lord St Levan teeing up at Pau in France. Pau Golf Club claims to be the oldest on mainland Europe, started in 1856. Lord St Levan became a keen golfer and was a founding member of the West Cornwall Golf Club at Lelant, the first club to be established in Cornwall. In this picture, he is with friends and family. He and his wife, Elizabeth had thirteen children, six boys in a row and then seven girls. The young boy in a brown suit and broad cream coloured hat is his youngest son, Lionel, who I remember as an old man. Great great uncle Lion, as he was known, was a tremendously popular figure among his younger relations.

The two girls in Victorian sailing costumes in the pictures to the left of the golfing scene are daughters of Lord St Levan.

Beyond in the alcove is a miniature portrait of the 5th Sir John St Aubyn in his uniform at Westminster School at the age of 15 or 16. The sketch of a Mount boatman in traditional dress was painted by the Earl of St Germans while he was staying on the island.

There are a number of interesting snuff boxes and other amusing objets d'art in the showcase. One circular snuff box features a stook of hay using the hair of the ubiquitous 5th Sir John. The mementos of Napoleon were a gift from my uncle Giles, the youngest brother in his generation. Giles was a longstanding schoolmaster at Eton College, being Head of the History Department for many years. He has also written several biographies and other books, especially about 19th century subject matter.

As you leave the Smoking Room onto the South Terrace, make sure (if the weather is at all reasonable) that you turn right to look down over the south side at the formal gardens.

1.

2.

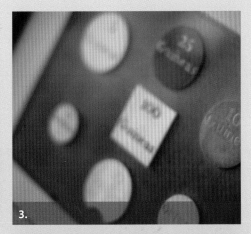

3.

4.

Opposite page – Golfing picture
Lord St Levan prepares to drive.

1 & 2 – Mother of perl chest
The chest, inlaid with mother of perl, came from Zanzibar. It is said to have belonged to the Duke of Parma and ejected through a window of his house during the revolution of 1859 when the Duke was driven out.

3 – Gambling counters
A set of seven counters for amounts between half a guinea to one hundred guineas used at Brooks's Club in St James's Street from its foundation in 1764. The 5th Sir John was a regular patron, and his portrait still hangs in Brooks's today.

4 – Napoleon mementos
These include a fragment of the coat Napoleon wore at the battle of Waterloo.

South Terrace and North Terrace

You are now on the roof of the East Wing where we live. There was a much smaller terrace here before the great Victorian building project between 1873 and 1878. The East Wing is built against a precipice within the rock structure, which is how it comes to be lower than the earlier buildings on the summit.

Lord St Levan employed his first cousin, Piers St Aubyn, as his architect, and this is undoubtedly the latter's masterpiece. Piers St Aubyn was a prolific church architect, but John Betjeman for one was subsequently very critical that his sometimes drastic renovations were too brutal. He missed the commission to build Truro Cathedral by a single vote.

As you look over the south wall, there is an almost sheer drop of some 200 feet to the formal gardens below. These are designed to be seen from above as well as from ground level, and this is another challenge to our gardening team to add to salt air, storm force winds and the abseiling skills they require to reach some of the more inaccessible areas of the garden. On the other hand, plants on this southern curve of the island gain exposure to a fantastic amount of light, while the mother rock of the Mount absorbs heat during the day and releases it at night, creating microclimates in which wonderfully exotic and unexpected succulents can flourish. This is truly gardening on the edge.

The walled garden was initiated around 1780 by the four Miss St Aubyns who were sisters of the 5th Sir John.

The surrounding terraces were created as part of the Victorian building project. On days when the gardens are open, you will find the entrance by the Island Café.

The turret, which you can walk round, is at the top of the granite spiral staircase which connects all the floors in the East Wing. My children's skateboards and jumps are sometimes spotted just inside the door, as after hours the terrace makes a good surface for skateboarding.

As you make your way to the North Terrace, you follow the walkway round the Blue Drawing Room. This is a mid eighteenth century restoration on the footprint of an earlier Lady Chapel. The earliest mention of this is a reference in 1430 to *a Chapel of blessed Marie* and it is then described by William of Worcester after his visit in 1478 as *newly built,* which suggests that a rebuild of the earlier structure had occurred. The motive for building the Lady Chapel may have been at least partly commercial. Pilgrimage in the Middle Ages would have had a significant impact on the priory's finances and the wider local economy, with the need to provide lodging and food for travellers, as well as the opportunity to sell them potions, mementos and relics.

As the Virgin Mary became increasingly significant within popular religious culture, it would have helped to continue to attract pilgrims to have a chapel dedicated to her.

William Borlase, Rector of Ludgvan from 1722 until his death in 1772, was a well known Cornish antiquarian and writer.

He had been a contemporary of the 3rd Sir John St Aubyn at Exeter College, Oxford, and he remained a firm friend of the family. He described a visit to the Mount in 1731, when *the roof of the Lady Chapel was lately fallen and walls crack'd in so many places that its own weight must needs bring it down in little time.* It seems that the original building did indeed fall down, but by 1762 Borlase was able to give a detailed description of the reconstructed Blue Drawing Room with the interior much as it is today.

The stone lion on the North Terrace was brought from Egypt by the 2nd Lord St Levan and is believed to have been made about 400 BC. As you look at the wall of the church, you can see the highest point of the bedrock protruding at its base.

Looking west, past Smoking Room

King Charles Room (upper floor)

Left – Photograph of 1st Lord & Lady St Levan and their grandchildren
My own grandfather is the boy on the extreme left.

Did you know?

That Charles II, when Prince of Wales, slept in the top room on the left before fleeing to the Isles of Scilly in 1646.

Church of St Michael & All Angels

You have now reached the beating heart of St Michael's Mount. On the footprint of the church built in 1135, and probably reusing the same stones, the present building was largely rebuilt in the late fourteenth century. In all likelihood, there would have been an earlier church still on the summit, but no remains are identifiable. There is a tradition that St Cadoc and St Keyne met on the island in the sixth century.

1.

2.

1. Lantern Cross
King, possibly Edward the Confessor. There is an entry in the records at Mont-St-Michel that Edward the Confessor, whose mother was Norman, had given them the Mount, but this is generally considered a forgery. On the other hand. Edward, who was canonised in 1161, was for almost two hundred years the patron saint of England.

2. Alabaster – John the Baptist
Nottingham Alabaster showing the head of John the Baptist being received in Heaven. The three persons of the Trinity are at the top (Son, Holy Ghost, Father from left to right). Also represented are the Virgin Mary with infant, St Peter with book and key, St Christopher carrying our Lord across the water, St James the Great with a pilgrim's hat and an Archbishop, again possibly Thomas Becket.

3. Alabaster – Pontius Pilate
Nottingham Alabaster showing Pontius Pilate washing his hands.

4. West window
Window added in the fifteenth century, although the stained glass is early twentieth century.

The Mount therefore has been a destination for pilgrims for a very long time indeed, and many visitors still experience a spiritual uplift when they come to this special place. We have our own Chaplain and visiting organist. We hold services on Christmas Day, Good Friday, Easter Sunday and every Sunday from Whit Sunday until the end of September. We also have a special service on St Michael's Day on 29th September, which is usually very well attended.

A document pupporting to be issued by Pope Gregory VII in 1070 granted St Michael's Mount freedom from episcopal jurisdiction. There is good reason to doubt whether this supposed edict was authentic. Nevertheless the church remains to this day independent of the diocese of Truro.

The organ was built by John Avery of Bristol in 1786 for Colonel John Lemon, MP for Truro for his London house in Bryanston Square. Apparently Colonel Lemon was an insomniac and during his wakeful spells would find relief by playing his organ at all hours of the night. Eventually his neighbours complained so vociferously that he was persuaded to sell the organ to his friend John St Aubyn for £800. Over the years the organ has been restored a number of times, but on no occasion have any tonal alterations been made so that it retains its original superb tonal quality.

The Lantern Cross is fifteenth century. It is made from Cornish stone from near Padstow, and may well have been commissioned for the Lady Chapel. It was probably kept inside until in 1827 the pinnacles were added and it was placed on the stone balcony at the top of the steps at the entrance to the church.

In 2008, the decision was taken to bring it inside once more to avoid any further erosion from exposure to the weather. The four panels represent the crucifixion, the virgin and child, a king (possibly Edward the Confessor who is often associated with the Mount) and a priest (who may be a prior or perhaps Thomas Becket).

The gilt chandelier was introduced in 1788 by the 5th Sir John St Aubyn It is a replica of a fifteenth century Flemish chandelier then in Temple Church, Bristol, now in Bristol Cathedral. The original has a figure of St George, but this version has had wings added to transform it to a figure of St Michael. As you can imagine, it is something of a performance to light the candles on the chandelier, but we do so at Christmas.

The modern bronze figure of St Michael defeating Lucifer, yet offering the hand of mercy, was made by the figurative sculptor, Lyn Constable Maxwell. The neighbouring stained glass windows were probably installed by the 5th Sir John as part of his restoration of the church in 1811. The panels themselves date from the fifteenth to the seventeenth century. It is particularly worth noting the charming scene of a schoolboy playing with a knuckle-bone while his dog rummages in a basket. It was made in the 1490s and is probably Flemish.

The stained glass above the altar was installed in 1875, whilst that in the fifteenth century rose window by the organ was commissioned to commemorate the 1st Lord St Levan after his death in 1908.

The same firm of John J Jennings then gradually adorned the remaining windows on the south and north walls. When you come to the lectern, glance to your right where there is a touching image of the Virgin and child, with the Mount in the background and the family dog of the time in the foreground.

On the wall behind the altar are three alabaster panels made in Nottingham in the fifteenth century. The central one is especially fine, portraying the severed head of John the Baptist on a charger being received in heaven by the Holy Trinity and assorted saints. The panel would originally have been coloured but this has almost all gone. The image on the left represents the Mass of St Gregory, a medieval allegory which relates that St Gregory had come to doubt that communion bread really changed into the body of Jesus until his faith was restored by a vision of the crucified Christ. The final panel on the right shows Pontius Pilate washing his hands.

Above the alabasters is a Crucifix carved by John Miller, who was better known for his paintings of landscapes and seascapes. It was given by him to the church in 1987. It was the first woodcarving that John had ever made. When it was done, he wrote a lovely letter to Lord St Levan describing his creative experience in producing the work. Part of it describes the piece – *The feet and legs speak of vulnerability and the torso and arms of love. The head is that of everyman and, I hope, would not seem too far away for most nationalities.* Personally, I love the juxtaposition of ancient and modern between the Nottingham alabasters and the Crucifix.

If you peer over the stalls to your right, you will see the entrance to a small underground chamber. At the time of the restoration in 1720, it had been blocked up.

When workmen rediscovered the cell, they were astonished to find a very tall skeleton, together with the black jug that was hanging in Chevy Chase. Nobody knows who the person was, or whether their end was fair or foul. The other extraordinary thing is that the skeleton seems to be growing – when I was a boy he was seven foot, but I recently heard him described as seven foot ten!

When the church was first built, it may be that there was a natural fissure in the rock into which a small chamber could be constructed. Possibly the monks kept some of their sacred artifacts here. Inventories of the priory's possessions exist from the years of 1337, 1430 and 1535. Especially once St Michael's Mount was released from the need to send most of its income to France, its store of treasures and relics became quite considerable (until of course they were all confiscated during the dissolution of monasteries). A particular draw for pilgrims would have been the jawbone of St Apollonia. She was a virgin martyr in Alexandria, Egypt in 249 and was tortured by having her teeth pulled out one by one. As a result she became the patron saint of dentists and for those suffering from toothache, no doubt a common complaint in medieval times.

Bronze figure of St Michael

John Miller Crucifix

Detail of stained glass window

25

Blue Drawing Room

The Vestibule to the Blue Drawing Room was added during the mid eighteenth century conversion of the previous Lady Chapel. The four chairs are Gothic Chippendale and the coats-of-arms are those of the St Aubyn and Wingfield families. The 4th Sir John, who was responsible for the creation of this Blue Drawing Room suite around 1750, was married to Elizabeth Wingfield.

The busts by the window are of the 5th Sir John (in 1812) and his eventual wife, Juliana (in 1806). They are by Joseph Nollekens, widely regarded as the finest English sculptor at the time. His other sitters included George III, William Pitt the Younger and Charles James Fox.

The main Blue Drawing Room is a fine example of the Strawberry Hill Gothick or Rococo style. It is utterly surprising to find here in a remote house in Cornwall such a cutting edge example of this new fashion pioneered by Horace Walpole. He was the youngest son of Robert Walpole and a cousin of Lord Nelson, and is mainly remembered for reviving the gothic style, especially in the architecture of his own home, Strawberry Hill in Twickenham.

About once every thirty years, the room is repainted using the same mix and shade of blue, which then gradually darkens until the next application. This was most recently done in 2006.

The five chairs in this room (and there are another five in the smaller room beyond) are particularly fine, being Chippendale from around 1755. The blue sofa is from a different set, but is also notable because Queen Victoria sat on it. In 1846, she and

Prince Albert were holidaying off the coast of Cornwall in the Royal Yacht of the day, when they decided to make a relatively impromptu visit to St Michael's Mount. The family were absent at the time and the Queen was shown round the castle by the housekeeper, Thomasina Sims. The visit seems to have been a success, and in her diary, Queen Victoria described Thomasina as *a nice, tidy little woman*. You can see an imprint of the Queen's tiny foot if you leave the harbour from the far steps.

The paintings above the door are by Thomas Hudson of the 4th Sir John and his wife Elizabeth, while the family group above the fireplace shows them with (I think) her mother and their five children, the 5th Sir John and his four sisters. The pictures on the north and south walls are of the 5th Sir John and his first cousin and friend, Francis Bassett, first Lord Dunstanville. The story goes that the two decided to exchange portraits, but an element of competition crept in, so that Francis Bassett was painted by Gainsborough and Sir John by Reynolds, the two leading artists of their day. The Bassett family still own the Reynolds while we have the Gainsborough. The picture here of Sir John is a copy of the Reynolds by the Cornish artist, John Opie.

The 5th Sir John was an early and lifelong patron of Opie. He was the leading pall-bearer at Opie's funeral in St Paul's Cathedral, and quite possibly sponsored the whole occasion. At a young age, Opie had been launched on fashionable London by his mentor Dr John Wolcot of Truro as the Cornish Wonder. Wolcot (who also wrote racy satires under the pen-name Peter Pindar) rather misleadingly suggested that Opie was able to paint without any previous tuition. After sensational initial success, Opie's crude country manners and still not fully developed style on canvas meant that he soon fell from favour. Nevertheless he continued to work with great determination to improve his technique, leading his rival Northcote to remark *"Other artists paint to live: Opie lives to paint"*. In time his career progressed and in 1805, he was appointed Professor of Painting at the Royal Academy. His annual lectures in this role showed an incisive understanding of art, and were published in 1809, the year he died aged 45.

The red jasper and white marble vases in the recesses either side of the door were brought from Italy when the room was rebuilt. The pair of giltwood pier tables under the Italian vases are a composite of mid 18th century serpentine veined yellow marble tops on later pierced columns. However the console table under the portrait of the 5th Sir John is pure George II.

One of pair of 18th century Italian red jasper and white marble vases

One of four Gothick Chippendale chairs

One of set of ten Chippendale chairs

Figure representing industry, her counterpart idleness, on French mantel clock. About 1880

Map Room, Staircase & Long Passage

The maps in the Map Room date back to the late sixteenth century. To your right as you enter is a charming map by William Holes (1612) which shows the whereabouts of various giants who by legend once occupied the high hills of Cornwall. Notice also the map by the window by Christopher Saxton.

Saxton was commissioned by William Cecil, chief advisor to Elizabeth I, to survey the whole of England and Wales. The resulting maps set the standard for cartographers for well over a hundred years. As it happens, the Cecil family were the first private owners of St Michael's Mount.

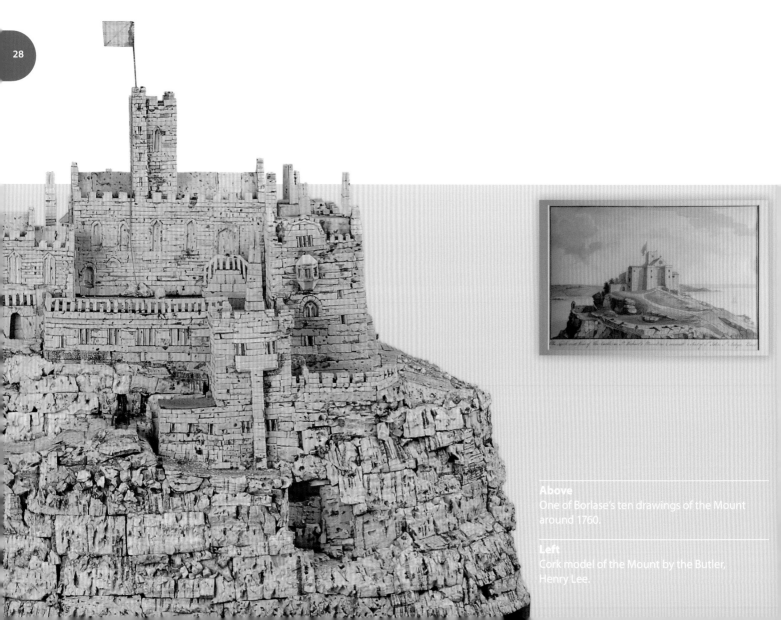

Above
One of Borlase's ten drawings of the Mount around 1760.

Left
Cork model of the Mount by the Butler, Henry Lee.

The model of the Mount was made out of champagne corks by Henry Lee, butler in the 1930s. In those days the family were accustomed to drinking champagne with their fish course so Lee would have had plenty of raw material. The model is beautifully to scale and as the geography of the castle can be somewhat confusing at first, it may help you to interpret its lay-out. In all, Henry Lee worked on the Mount for 49 years.

As you descend the stairs from the Map Room, you will meet three Lady St Levans. On the left is my aunt, Susan, painted by Carlos Sancha, and beneath her my grandmother, Gwen, painted by Rodrigo Moyniham. On the right is a bewitching portrait of Julia, second wife of the 2nd Lord St Levan, by Philip de Laszlo. It is said that Jack St Aubyn (as he then was) and Julia were sweethearts when young, but Julia's family apparently did not approve of him as a prospective suitor. Both married others but, after each had been widowed, they were finally united.

On your left is a large portrait of Sir Francis Bassett, who spent so much on fortifying the Mount during the Civil War. It is thought to be by Cornelius Janssens. Conventionally such a large picture should be hung in a bigger space, but I rather like the way it is possible to be close enough to see its detail.

On the right is Robert Walpole by Godfrey Kneller. This is one of several portraits in the castle purchased from Raynham, home of the Townshend family. The 1st Lord St Levan was married to Elizabeth Townshend and took the opportunity offered by the Raynham Sale of 1904 to acquire several pictures to fill the additional wall space that he had created by building the East Wing. Walpole's sister had also married a Townshend. Rather amusingly the picture nameplate identifies Walpole only as brother of Dorothy without mentioning his eminence as the first Prime Minister.

Looking back from the foot of the stairs, there is a portrait by Opie of Dolly Pentreath, who lived in nearby Mousehole and was the last person alive who only spoke the Cornish language. Opie was sixteen when he painted this and it can be seen that he was mimicking the style of Rembrandt. On the other side of the door are Mary and me on a landing in the East Wing of the castle. We were painted by Richard Foster with sittings in London and Cornwall over many months. It was fascinating to watch as the portrait gradually came together.

The Long Passage was created as part of the renovations of 1780, as most likely was the Map Room. There are numerous prints and drawings, including a number of Cornish houses, not all of which still exist, and six scenes from nineteenth century life at Eton College. There are also ten drawings of different aspects of the Mount by William Borlase, which provide a detailed record of the castle around 1760.

Dolly Pentreath by John Opie

Julia, Lady St Levan by Phillip de Laszio

Garrison Room and Exit

At the foot of the Kitchen Stairs, turn left into the Garrison Room where we house our armoury. Before you enter the room, there are two oriental polearms and a fearsome looking weapon in the corner. This is a sleeve entangler and was used by Japanese policemen to entrap fugitives by catching the folds of their kimonos.

Inside there is a magnificent Samurai suit of armour, which dates from about 1800. The subsequent period was a predominantly peaceful phase in Japanese history and it is likely that the armour was seen in procession rather than in battle. It was brought back from Japan by the 2nd Lord St Levan, who had accompanied Arthur, Duke of Connaught on the Garter Mission to Japan.

Samurai suit of armour

Arthur was a younger brother of Edward VII and had been deputed to invest the Mikado of Japan (Emperor) with the Order of the Garter. This unprecedented diplomatic initiative, which was extremely well received in Japan, was intended to cement the Anglo-Japanese Alliance first signed in 1902 and which was to last until 1923.

All the showcases in this room and indeed the rest of the castle have been made in our own estate workshops. The National Trust have advised us on the various displays, and in the case of this room arranged for an expert from the Royal Armouries in Leeds to come to assist us. All the exhibits have been brought back by members of the family, or islanders, from their military service or travels around the world. The central cabinet is arranged with English weapons on one side, segmented into the 17th to 20th centuries, and overseas weapons, mainly from Asia, on the other.

To me the most poignant part of the collection is at the far end of the room.

This contains the helmet worn in the trenches during the First World War by my grandfather. He was wounded by a bullet in the neck, which at the time must have seemed a misfortune, but in retrospect may have removed him from worse danger. The red beret was worn by my father at Arnhem, where he was one of the few officers to return home. For his action there he was awarded the MC, but possibly not for his habit of reading Trollope during lulls in the battle, as a means to exude calm to his men. The German officer's ceremonial dagger was somehow acquired by one of the Mount gardeners and donated to the collection.

As you leave towards the exit, you pass through a tunnel going underneath the Church. Like the Kitchen Stairs, this is part of the great Victorian works, as was the creation of new kitchens at the far end of the tunnel. By the time food had made its way from the kitchen to Chevy Chase, it may have been less than piping hot. The former Kitchen is now opened periodically when we show an exhibition which is relevant to the Mount.

Just before you reach the exit, there is a saddle which came from Buffalo Bill's Wild West Show which, during a two year tour of the UK covering 132 cities and towns, played to a huge crowd at Penzance in 1904. The Show contained Chief Iron Tail and his Sioux Indians, cowboys, Mexicans, Japanese, US cavalry and artillery, as well as various celebrities. When Colonel Cody – or Buffalo Bill – visited the Mount, he is meant to have compared the freshness of the air to what he knew back home.

Outside the exit door are some elegant cannons captured from a French frigate disabled by fire from the Mount during the Napoleonic War. At Mont-St-Michel, they have some captured English guns so you could say that honours are even between England and France on this front.

I hope that you have been entertained on your tour, and that you have time to experience some of the other facilities on the island. Many visitors come to see us again, and if you are not already among their number, I hope that you may be tempted to return before too long.

Cowboy saddle from Buffalo Bill's Circus

Buffalo Bill on the Mount in 1904

French cannon detail

French cannon

Timeline of St Michael's Mount

Approx 275 Million years ago

The Mount was created when the Cornubian Batholith was formed following the cooling of magma or molten rock resulting from the collision of the earth's tectonic plates. The batholith is the granite spine, rich in minerals, that runs most of the length of Devon and Cornwall. It would originally have been some 10,000 metres beneath the earth's surface, but in several places, including St Michael's Mount, long term erosion has left the granite exposed.

Mesolithic Age or Middle Stone Age (7000 – 4000 BC)

It is possible, even likely, that the hunter gatherers of this period would have used the Mount as a periodic base, if not as a more permanent camp. A flint arrowhead has been found on the island, which may date from this period.

Neolithic Age or New Stone Age (4000 – 2000 BC)

It has been suggested that the Mount could have been a hilltop enclosure controlling an extensive territory in West Penwith, similar to what is known to have existed at Carn Brea, near Redruth.

c2000 BC

Until now a marshy forest, Mount's Bay was inundated by the sea, and the Mount became a tidal island.

Bronze Age (2000 – 800 BC)

It is almost inconceivable that the Mount would not have been a significant centre during the Bronze Age, but only very recently has the discovery of artifacts from the latter part of this period confirmed that there was activity on the island then.

Early Iron Age (800 – 400 BC)

Archaeology carried out in 1998 during the installation of a new sewer pipe identified six platforms for roundhouses of the sort prevalent in Cornwall at this time. The sites are surprisingly close together, which may indicate that a larger overall settlement existed.

Ictis (400 BC – 400 AD)

Diodorus Siculus, a Greek historian in the first century BC, compiled the Bibliotheca historica, drawing on many earlier sources. In this, he describes how tin was worked in Ancient Britain, then transported to a tidal island called Ictis where merchants would buy it, then sail to Gaul, before a 30 day overland journey to the mouth of the Rhone. Over the years, there has been much debate concerning the identity of Ictis, but much the most likely candidate is St Michael's Mount. It is possible that the Mount continued to operate as a port throughout the Romano-British period.

Dark Ages (400 – 1000)

It has been speculated that in the early part of this period the island may have housed a citadel similar to Tintagel, or else an early Christian centre. There is a medieval account of a supposed meeting between St Cadoc and St Keyne on the Mount in the sixth century. Other iconic sites dedicated to St Michael were established across Western Europe especially in the latter half of this period, and it is reasonable to suppose that by then a religious community might have gathered here. The 1998 Archaeological Survey discovered a Christian grave, whose bones were carbon dated to a mid-point of 900, adding some physical evidence of a possible pre-Norman monastery.

c1080

Grant by Robert, Count of Mortain, of St Michael's Mount to Mont-St-Michel. Robert was a half-brother of William the Conqueror and following the Norman Conquest was made Earl of Cornwall. It is not clear whether his charter was a generous gift or – perhaps more in keeping with his character – an attempt to re-balance in his favour the property belonging to him and that which previously had already been in the possession of Mont-St-Michel.

1135

Work started to build the Church by authority of Abbot, Bernard Le Bec, of Mont-St-Michel.

1144

Church consecrated by Robert, Bishop of Exeter.

1193

Henry de la Pomeray seized the Mount. He was an ally of Prince John, later King John, who was making overtures to replace his brother, Richard I, on the throne while the latter was held captive on the continent. On Richard's return, John sought and received pardon but de la Pomeray refused to surrender the Mount. Thereupon Richard I sent a considerable force under the command of Hubert Walter, his influential advisor who variously held the posts of Archbishop of Canterbury, Chief Justice and Lord Chancellor. In the face of hopeless odds, de la Pomeray caused himself to be bled to death, an action which under the law of the time made sure that his Will was valid – and this included a bequest to the monks of St Michael's Mount.

1275

Earthquake on the Mount mentioned in the Annals of Waverley, an important medieval source document. If correct, this is presumably the same powerful earthquake which is known to have destroyed St Michael's Church at Glastonbury and many other buildings on 11 September that year.

1385

Richard Auncell of Tavistock installed by Richard II as prior. He was the first non-French prior, indicating how Mont-St-Michel's control was steadily being relinquished through the Hundred Years War with France.

1414

By Act of Parliament, Henry V was empowered to appropriate the alien priories including St Michael's Mount, which he transferred to his new foundation, the Bridgettine convent of Syon Abbey.

1442

Henry VI granted St Michael's Mount to King's College, Cambridge, which he had founded the previous year.

1461

When the Yorkist Edward IV overthrew the Lancastrian Henry VI, he promptly returned St Michael's Mount to Syon Abbey.

1473

John de Vere, 13th Earl of Oxford, captured the Mount and with a force of only 80 withstood a siege of 26 weeks against the King's army of 6,000 fighting men. One of the Lancastrian commanders defeated at the battle of Barnet, Oxford's intentions at the time are unclear, although he did have Cornish connections and may have hoped for more local support. After his surrender in 1474, Oxford was imprisoned in the fortress at Hammes, near Calais. He eventually escaped to the court of Henry Tudor and in 1485 played a decisive role in the latter's victory at the Battle of Bosworth.

1497

Katherine, wife of Perkin Warbeck, stayed for safety at St Michael's Mount as her husband, who claimed to be one of the Princes in the Tower who had survived, raised an army in Cornwall to march to replace Henry VII on the throne. Perkin failed and was forced to confess himself an imposter – to which Katherine is meant to have said that it *was the man and not the king she loved.*

1535

Inventory of priory goods as preparations for the dissolution of monasteries were underway. The last clergy on the Mount were pensioned off in 1548.

1549

The Book of Common Prayer was introduced, presenting the theology of the English Reformation. The proposal to hold services in English was particularly badly received in West Cornwall, where most of the inhabitants spoke only Cornish. At the outset of the ensuing Prayer Book Rebellion, several local gentry took refuge in St Michael's Mount, but to no avail as the rebels successfully besieged the castle and took the gentlemen and their wives as hostages. In the end, as another Cornish uprising petered out, the hostages were released unharmed.

1588

Spanish Armada spotted as it passed Mount's Bay, and beacon lit at the top of the Church tower, the first of a chain set up all along the south coast of England to alert London of the Armada's arrival.

1599

Elizabeth I sold St Michael's Mount to her chief advisor, Robert Cecil, later Earl of Salisbury.

Timeline of St Michael's Mount

continued

1640

Mount sold by 2nd Earl of Salisbury to Sir Francis Bassett of Tehidy. Sir Francis spent large sums fortifying the Mount between 1642 and 1645. He died in September that year, and his brother Arthur surrendered the Mount in 1646 to avoid unnecessary loss of blood once the Royalist cause was clearly lost.

1659

Colonel John St Aubyn purchased the Mount from the son of Sir Francis Bassett.

1720

The 3rd Sir John St Aubyn repaired the Church and in 1726/7 rebuilt the harbour, which led to the revitalization of the village over the next century.

1755

Extensive damage in the harbour area of St Michael's Mount and around the rest of Mount's Bay from a 3 metre tsunami caused by the Great Lisbon Earthquake on 1st November. This was a huge earthquake which destroyed 85% of the buildings in Lisbon with great loss of life. As well as its physical impact, the scale of the disaster initiated considerable philosophical debate throughout Europe whether this was a message from an angry God.

1812

French privateer dismasted by cannon fire from the southeast battery and its guns captured as it was forced ashore on Marazion beach.

1846

Queen Victoria and Prince Albert visited while on holiday. In the absence of the family, they were shown round by the housekeeper, Mrs Sims.

1873

Work started to build the East Wing and to renovate many parts of the existing castle. Piers St Aubyn's design has been described by Nigel Nicolson as among the greatest achievements of 19th century architecture.

1902

Edward VII visited St Michael's Mount. This time the family were forewarned and indeed Lord St Levan lent his barge for the King's use while he was in the Isles of Scilly.

1954

The 3rd Lord St Levan gave most of St Michael's Mount to the National Trust, but retained a 999 year lease for the St Aubyn family to live in the castle together with a licence to run the visitor business on the island.

2004

Tradition of renovation continued as 5 year programme started to replace all electric wiring, the plumbing and other services in the castle as well as re-pointing most of the exterior walls and renewing the roofs.

The castle today

A plan of the Castle showing the layout of most of the rooms covered in this guide.

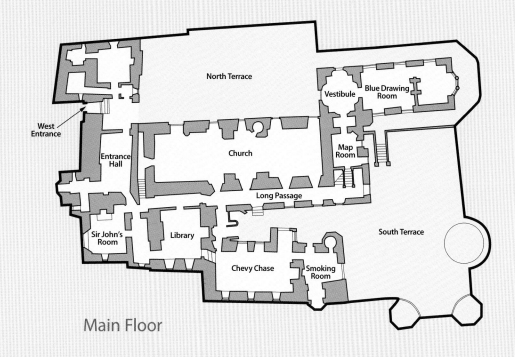

Main Floor

The castle as it was

A plan of the Castle showing the likely layout of the rooms in the early sixteenth Century.

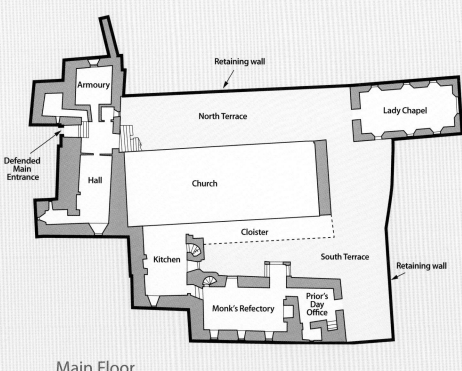

Main Floor

St Aubyn family who have lived on the Mount

Beside is the line of succession of members of the St Aubyn family who have lived on St Michael's Mount – many of whose portraits can be seen during your visit.

Colonel John St Aubyn (1610 – 1684)

m. Catherine Godolphin
Purchased the Mount in 1659

Sir John St Aubyn (1645 – 1699)

m. Ann Jenkyn
Created a Baronet in 1671

Sir John St Aubyn (1669 – 1714)

m. Mary de la Hay
Second Baronet

Sir John St Aubyn (1700 – 1744)

m. Catherine Morice
Third Baronet

Sir John St Aubyn (1726 – 1772)

m. Elizabeth Wingfield
Fourth Baronet

Sir John St Aubyn (1758 – 1839)

m. Juliana Vinnecombe
Fifth Baronet

James St Aubyn (1783 – 1862)

m. Sarah White
Baronetcy became extinct as parents unmarried

Sir Edward St Aubyn (1799 – 1872)

m. Emma Knollys
Created a Baronet in 1866

John, Lord St Levan (1829 – 1908)

m. Lady Elizabeth Townshend
Created a Baron in 1887

John, Lord St Levan (1857 – 1940)

m. (1) Lady Edith Edgcumbe,
(2) Julia Wombwell
Second Baron

Francis, Lord St Levan (1895 – 1978)

m. Gwendolen Nicolson
Third Baron

John, Lord St Levan (1919 –)

m. Susan Kennedy
Fourth Baron. Retired to the mainland in 2003

James St Aubyn (1950 –)

m. Mary Bennett
Currently living in the castle

Right
St Aubyn family photograph.